Gatsby, **GATH, and Gault**

The Influence of *The Entailed Hat*
on *The Great Gatsby*

David W. Meredith

Bloomington, IN  Milton Keynes, UK

AuthorHouse™
1663 Liberty Drive, Suite 200
Bloomington, IN 47403
www.authorhouse.com
Phone: 1-800-839-8640

AuthorHouse™ UK Ltd.
500 Avebury Boulevard
Central Milton Keynes, MK9 2BE
www.authorhouse.co.uk
Phone: 08001974150

© 2007 David W. Meredith. All rights reserved.

No part of this book may be reproduced, stored in a retrieval system, or transmitted by any means without the written permission of the author.

First published by AuthorHouse 9/13/2007

ISBN: 978-1-4259-9278-1 (sc)

Printed in the United States of America
Bloomington, Indiana

This book is printed on acid-free paper.

George Alfred Townsend is a name that was well known in America in 1900 but is known hardly at all today. It is most familiar to natives of Delaware and Maryland's Eastern Shore, who know him if at all by his pen-name "GATH." Gath, they will say, wrote a book about Patty Cannon, a notorious slave trader who lived early in the nineteenth century in a house that straddled the Maryland/Delaware line. Civil War buffs who have been to Harper's Ferry and Antietam might have heard of Gath as a newspaper reporter who covered battles during the American Civil War and later in life built a monument to war correspondents on his estate west of Frederick, Maryland. They might have heard of—and even read—a novel he wrote that recounts the Lincoln assassination and its aftermath and is based on his own personal on-the-scene observations. Some very few might know too that he published poems, short stories, and essays, and wrote a nationally syndicated newspaper column during the late nineteenth and early twentieth centuries, and they might even have heard that at the turn of the century there was a cigar named after him (Shields 1-48).

I believe that F. Scott Fitzgerald knew who Townsend was and had read at least one of his works, a romantic novel called *The Entailed Hat*. I believe he discussed this book seriously with a college friend of his, John Biggs, Jr., and that discussions of the book with Biggs were a significant influence on Fitzgerald in conceiving *The Great Gatsby*. In the essay that follows, I attempt to demonstrate likenesses between *The Great Gatsby* and *The Entailed Hat* sufficient, I think, to show that Fitzgerald had read this romantic history and was influenced by it. In addition, I hope to show convincingly that not only *Gatsby*, published by Scribner in 1925, but also John Biggs's novel *Demigods*, published by Scribner in 1926, alludes to *The Entailed Hat* and to facts about the life of its writer, George Alfred Townsend. My aim is not at all to diminish Fitzgerald's achievement in *Gatsby*. He exaggerated only slightly, I believe, when he remarked to Maxwell Perkins about *Gatsby* in 1924, "I think that at last I've done something really my own" (Turnbull 188). Taking as his cue certain themes, situations, devices, and characters from *The Entailed Hat*, he achieved effect and significance in *The Great Gatsby* beyond what he had achieved in his two earlier novels, and he did this in his own distinctive voice.

Where and when Fitzgerald read *The Entailed Hat* I can only speculate. It might have been at home in Minnesota, or maybe at prep school, or at

Princeton, or perhaps in Delaware in 1924 or 1925. But there is good reason to believe he had access to this novel. And there is especially good reason to think it was fresh in his mind while he was fishing for inspiration for a new project of his own. One recommendation for believing that *Hat* was a source is that it was written by someone who, like himself, had roots in Maryland. Fitzgerald was proud to be descended in the line of Francis Scott Key, after whom his parents had named him, and would rather have been associated with his Maryland background than with Minnesota, where he was born.[1] If he had not read *The Entailed Hat* earlier than 1924, he likely came to know it through his Princeton friend John Biggs, Jr., whose grandfather had been a governor of Delaware, whose father was Delaware's attorney general, and whose family had possibly known the Townsends early in the nineteenth century.[2]

George Alfred Townsend's own family roots were in both Maryland and Delaware. His mother's family was from Somerset and Worcester Counties, where *Hat* is set, and Townsend's father was a Methodist minister whose church had moved him from one parish in the area to another every few years. The route of these assignments took the family from Maryland up the Delmarva Peninsula and eventually to an area near Philadelphia.[3] In Delaware and in Pennsylvania Townsend attended superior schools and by age twenty was employed writing for a Philadelphia newspaper. Over the next few decades he traveled in America and Europe and by middle age was a sophisticated, analytical man of the world. Memories of his childhood led him in mid-life to go back to Delmarva for a while to get in touch with his background. Researching his mother's genealogy while he was there, he discovered mention of a hat that had been entailed in her family, and this set his imagination to work.[4] At the end of this extended sentimental journey, he wrote a novel concerned with American values, using the entailed hat as its central symbol.

Though he was not born in Maryland, Fitzgerald had visited there, and from time to time during his life he lived at various locations in Maryland and in Delaware. For parts of two years during the twenties, he and Zelda lived north of Wilmington in a grand old mansion called "Ellerslie" that John Biggs arranged for them to lease. Gradually, Maryland became the itinerant Fitzgerald's chosen "home," and John Biggs remained his friend for life. Like Fitzgerald, Biggs had shown considerable talent as a writer at Princeton, and he continued writing after he went on to Harvard Law School. Though he published two novels during the last half of the twenties, he established himself as an attorney in Delaware and was later appointed as a judge on the Third Circuit Court of Appeals.[5]

While at Princeton, however, he consorted with a coterie of writers that included Edmund Wilson and John Peale Bishop. He and Fitzgerald were both on the staff of the Princeton *Lit* and the *Nassau Tiger*, which they sometimes wrote entirely by themselves, sometimes working through the night to meet deadlines.[6] During the decade following his years at Princeton and Harvard, Biggs wrote several short stories and had two novels published by Scribner (*Demigods* in 1926 and *Seven Days Whipping* in 1928). Like Fitzgerald, he worked with Scribner's talented editor Maxwell Perkins. So far as I know, he published no other novels. During the 1930's he agreed to act as literary executor for Fitzgerald and served in that capacity after Fitzgerald's death in 1940.

Quite possibly it was through Biggs that Fitzgerald came to know *The Entailed Hat*. From a letter he wrote to Biggs in 1939, it appears that the two of them often recommended to each other works that they liked and traded opinions about

5

them, as Fitzgerald and Edmund Wilson also often did. If Fitzgerald had not read a copy of *Hat* owned by his father in Minnesota or by Biggs at Princeton, he might have read it elsewhere. Whatever the case, it seems certain to me that he and Biggs had read and discussed Townsend's novel together before 1924, when Fitzgerald was writing *The Great Gatsby*, and 1926, when Biggs's *Demigods* was published by Scribner.[7] Someone who has read all three of these books cannot help but think *The Entailed Hat* inspired both of them to efforts of their own.

Gatsby and *Demigods* are very different in style but share two central concerns: to trace the progress of their protagonists towards adult personal identity, and to depict the effects on them of America's code of personal values. *The Entailed Hat* also focuses on the conflict in American life between traditional Christian morality and America's steadily evolving material ethos. Biggs and Fitzgerald both project this dilemma and dramatize the difficulty and frustration their protagonists have in dealing with it. I suggest it was an aim of both of them to update and re-present these issues about personal and social identity for a contemporary readership. In doing this, they restyled Townsend's critique for their own generation, each in his own voice.

Though *The Entailed Hat* is stylistically uneven and flawed, it is interesting psychologically, sociologically, and historically. One flaw is its length, which Townsend and his editors did, indeed, see as a fault. He tells us in a footnote that his publisher required him to shorten the draft he first submitted, and adds, "In the original manuscript a circumstantial story, as taken from Milburn's lips, was preserved. The 'Tales of a Hat' may be separately published" (68). Another problem is its structure. About halfway through the book, Townsend shifts focus in a way that disunifies the plot. For twenty-one chapters he has focused on the career of a man named Meshach Milburn. In Chapter Twenty-Two, he shifts the action to a different locale and for most of the next twenty-two chapters abandons Milburn while he details the activities of a notorious gang of slave traders. Only then does he tie up the ends of the primary plot. Townsend refocuses on Milburn in the last two chapters of the book and in part of one other chapter along the way. But the novel's effect has been disunified. Townsend was aware of this fault and apologizes for it in his introduction. He explains that the story he began to tell "broke from its confines . . . and sought a larger hemisphere" (xiv). Indeed, many readers of the book remember the subplot more vividly than they do the main plot.

A third problem of *The Entailed Hat* concerns its uneven prose style. In some passages and to some ends it is very effective. For example, Townsend liberally uses dialogue instead of narration to sketch-in background and portray character. This gives drama and realism to the text, especially when he portrays local dialect, which he does often and aptly. However, some of the dialogue is melodramatic, and some of the narrative is turgid, even by nineteenth-century standards. But there are also narrative passages, especially in the early chapters, that echo the prose style of Hawthorne, whose writing Townsend admired. [8]

Fitzgerald was certainly not drawn to *The Entailed Hat* by its style.[9] It is very different from that of *Gatsby*. But induced most likely by John Biggs to read it, he must have found themes, elements of setting, and details there that inspired him. The appeal of Fitzgerald's first two novels had been to readers of his own age facing the social reality of his own generation. Of his performance in these novels, Edmund Wilson wrote, "[Fitzgerald] has been given imagination without intellectual control of it . . . and he has been given a gift for expression without many ideas to express" (Kazin 77). In *Gatsby* Fitzgerald looks piercingly at his surroundings and provides not just a portrait of modern manners and mores, but dramatizes what he feels about the nature of contemporary American values. In the book's last paragraphs, he provides historical perspective for his readers to use in abstracting the story's themes.

Nick Carraway, through whose eyes we see Gatsby and the scene against which his drama is portrayed, has returned to America from a war fought to preserve a set of values that by the end of the Gatsby saga he sees as naive. Like Rudolph Miller, the protagonist of "Absolution" whom Fitzgerald originally had in mind for Nick's role in *Gatsby*, Nick is effectually paralyzed by his insight. Fitzgerald cleverly gives Nick the story to tell in his own voice. For Nick it is an epiphany of human nature in action that leaves him spiritually inert.

When Fitzgerald began work on the book, he himself had had a taste of life that included battle, marriage, world travel, and drunken dissipation. He had gained insight into who ran the world and how. When he returned home, he was a bankrupt on the verge of becoming a cynic. Desperate for money and bereft of self confidence, he got a boost from being in touch again with John Biggs. I think that either then—in 1924—or maybe earlier, at Princeton, Fitzgerald and Biggs read and discussed *The Entailed Hat* together.[10] Considering the thematic similarities of *Gatsby* to certain features of Biggs's *Demigods* (published by Scribner in 1926), I think that discussions they had of Townsend's book and of Biggs's work-in-progress led Fitzgerald to conceive *Gatsby*. Perhaps he and Biggs even agreed to see what they both could do, each in his own style, to re-express a core theme of *The Entailed Hat*, the quest for personal identity.

Fitzgerald had begun this project with a protagonist who was very different from the Gatsby we meet early in the finished novel. In the first draft his protagonist is a young boy confused about the middling way of life he is being groomed to accept. But this character is completely different from the Gatsby that Fitzgerald writes about, though he might in certain respects have been a preliminary sketch of the middle-American character who becomes Nick Carraway. When Fitzgerald began work on *Gatsby*, he was still in touch with John Biggs. I tend to think that either then—in 1924, when he laid aside the prologue he had written for his third novel—or earlier, at Princeton, Fitzgerald and Biggs had read and discussed *The Entailed Hat* together. Considering the similarities of *Gatsby* and *Demigods* to each other, and of both of these to *The Entailed Hat*, it seems Fitzgerald and Biggs might even have agreed to see what they both could do, each in his own style, to re-express a core theme of *The Entailed Hat*, the quest for personal identity in America's modern industrial/capitalist society.

The Great Gatsby and *The Entailed Hat*

The Entailed Hat has been called a best-seller of its day, but these days a copy of it is hard to find except through inter-library loan or special order from a bookstore or via internet. As this book may not be readily available to all readers, I provide the following synopsis. In tandem with segments of the summary, I have indicated some of the borrowings that Fitzgerald seems to have made. Other borrowings I discuss following the synopsis.

The plot of *The Entailed Hat* concerns circumstances many of which actually took place in Maryland and Delaware during the 1820's and 1830's but which Townsend modified and rearranged in narrative time to suit the purposes of his story. Chief among these are the slave-trade activities of Patty Cannon and her gang, the operation of the Nassawongo Iron

Company in Worcester County, Maryland, and the competition between various industrial moguls to locate railway lines to their benefit. In the first half of his novel, Townsend demonstrates the quest for personal identity of Meshach Milburn, legatee of the entailed hat of the book's title. Born in the forest of Worcester County between Snow Hill and Princess Anne, he was orphaned at an early age by parents of mixed European and native-American stock. The sullen Milburn has used his wits to accumulate capital by various means, some of them revealed to his public and to the reader, and others left undisclosed. Fitzgerald portrays Gatsby as equally mysterious in this respect: the public at large seem not to know how he affords his elaborate lifestyle, and we readers are left almost equally in the dark.

Eventually, about four decades into his life, Milburn maneuvers the area's most influential citizen, Judge Daniel Custis, into granting him marriage to Vesta, his beautiful, virtuous daughter. Custis desperately needs money to avoid bankruptcy, and Milburn is able to provide it. In the course of his career, Milburn has by chance discovered he is descended from Jacob Milborne, an American patriot who in tandem with his father-in-law, Jacob Leisler, led a revolt against English economic oligarchy in

New York near the end of the seventeenth century. Leisler and Milborne were captured and hanged by the British but, ironically, several years later they were exonerated.[11] Meanwhile the remnants of the family had either migrated, or been forcibly displaced, to the lowlands of eastern Maryland and had sunk into poverty. This background is based on actual fact, it should be noted. And it should also be noted that the mother of Townsend himself was actually a Milborne. In researching his family history at the Snow Hill courthouse, Townsend came upon the following item in the will of one of his maternal ancestors: "'I give and bequeath to my Son, Ralph Milbourn, MY BEST HAT, TO HIM AND HIS ASSIGNEES FOREVER, and no more of my estate'" (Townsend xiii-xiv).

Discovering this connection with his own forebear led Meshach to locate and buy his ancestor's steeple-crown hat, which had remained in his family for over a century until his father had had to sell it for money to feed his family. Townsend has Meshach locate this outdated hat and wear it publicly on special occasions to nurture his self-esteem. But the result has been to make him a public laughing-stock. Importantly, Meshach's industry, cunning, and pride of origin are supplemented by the love that Vesta gradually develops for him after they are married. Her loyalty and understanding help to mellow his character and influence the use he makes of his growing fortune. In the book's final chapter, we find Milburn exhausted and dying after an unsuccessful project he launched to bolster Worcester County's economy: the extension of a railroad line south from Philadelphia and Wilmington to Princess Anne. Like Meshach's grotesque hat, Gatsby's gaudy mansion and roadster and entertainments are meant to rouse public notice and especially to please the woman he wants to marry. Both Meshach and Gatsby are ridiculous poseurs, each preening in his own way before a public whose good opinion he desires.

In the middle of *The Entailed Hat*, Townsend begins shifting attention from Meshach's career to other characters and other matters. With scant transition, he moves the plot's action up the Nanticoke River to a completely different setting and introduces a different set of characters than those we've been concerned with. Before long we find ourselves at the plantation of a vicious woman called Patty Cannon, who employs a gang of cut-throat scoundrels to kidnap black slaves and freedmen and smuggle them South to be sold at slave markets there. In this plot a young fisherman from Princess Anne named Levin

Dennis is persuaded to sail a suspicious stranger up the Nanticoke. In the course of the journey, Levin is overpowered by his passenger and cronies of his who have joined them. These are Patty Cannon's henchmen, we discover. Levin is threatened with death unless he joins their gang.

In *Gatsby* there is nothing quite like this divergent subplot. The action involving George and Myrtle Wilson and Tom Buchanan, though subordinate to Gatsby's quest, is integrated structurally with the main plot so that it does not really seem subordinate at all. And the storyline involving Nick and Jordan parallels the Gatsby/Daisy action so that it is more an intensifier of the main plot than a subplot. Nick Carraway is involved in all these actions in a special way: as a student of life, an as-yet uncommitted observer who will soon have to choose a model or develop a role for himself. In short, Fitzgerald's style is tight and economic, while Townsend's is loose and expansive. But both are dealing with the same general theme: the individual's development and practice of ethical values and personal identity in America's capitalistic society.

After weeks of travail, Levin is recognized by a man called Van Dorn, who is strategist of the brigands and also Patty Cannon's lover. Unbeknownst to

Levin, Van Dorn is actually his long-absent father, who has chosen this gypsy existence in preference to conventional village life with his family back in Princess Anne. Later, after having posed a life-or-death challenge to Levin designed to prove the worth of the young man's character, Van Dorn dies of a gunshot wound. Young Levin meanwhile demonstrates character to his father's satisfaction and ultimately returns to Princess Anne, marries, and takes his bride and his mother West with him where they will forge a new life for themselves. Soon after he leaves, Patty Cannon is captured and jailed and commits suicide in her jail cell before the law can get her to the gallows. Another line of action running through the second half of the novel involves the efforts of an ethically revived Daniel Custis and Delaware's Judge Clayton to defend the railroad project against monopoly by big-city business moguls. Additionally, the anti-slavery theme is portrayed both feelingly and melodramatically in the second half of the novel.

The two plotlines of *The Entailed Hat* are united by sharing several secondary characters and at least three central themes: the quest for personal identity, the evils of slavery, and the effects of materialism on the American character. In addition, Meshach

Milburn, protagonist of the first half of the novel, comes back into focus in the final chapters, providing the book with at least dramatic if not structural unity. Townsend found the lure of "local legends and truths about Patty Cannon" so irresistible because he had originally heard them from his mother when he was a child (Townsend x).

The steeple-crown hat is, of course, the central symbol of this romantic novel. Through it Townsend evokes the traits that Meshach's New York ancestors personified: their mercantile talent, for example, their mix of material and religious values, their obstinate independence, their determination, their bravery. These are traits he has inherited and illustrates in his behavior. However, as he lies dying, he ruminates about his life and decides not to wish on his son the stress and unhappiness his values have caused him. Rather than curse his son with remembering and perhaps living the sort of life he has led, he asks that the hat be buried with him (Townsend 565).

In reviewing the plot of *The Entailed Hat*, we have noted several correspondences between it and *The Great Gatsby*: (1) a central project of both of these novels is portraying the effects of American materialism on the values and outlooks of her citizens; (2) the protagonist in both novels courts public opinion by ostentatiously displaying his wealth and influence; (3) in both novels the protagonist's most immoral and illegal strategies for gaining wealth are not disclosed to the reader but merely intimated; and (4) both novels employ several subordinate lines of action to state or amplify the central theme. Let us consider these likenesses more fully, and add a few other correspondences, as well.

In America, status has historically been more often a product of risk, timing, manipulation, and chance than of hard manual work or inherited privilege. It was thus for Jimmy Gatz, who met Dan Cody at the right moment, and for Cody himself, who had been a prospector for precious metals. Meshach Milburn reached this conclusion, too, and gradually rose from abject poverty to wealth through cleverness and self-denial. And this was also the approach of his ancestor, Jacob Milborne, who for a while had out-maneuvered the British and French in New Amsterdam and his fellow-tradesmen, as well. The steeple-crown hat he left to his progeny implied the message that determination breeds success.

In *Gatsby*, the hat symbolism is subdued but present. Jimmy Gatz, a farm-boy from North Dakota with creative imagination, didn't need an antique hat to provide him a self-image. But he made his debut in the world of privilege under the brim of a yachting cap, and aboard Dan Cody's yacht he learned enough about status and power and their relation to wealth that he set out to become wealthy himself. After wartime service in the military, he made a quick fortune by dubious means and set himself up regally in a Long Island mansion. His yachting cap is not mentioned again in the novel, but it has been replaced by other symbols of affluence and power—everything from silk shirts and a grand piano to an elaborate roadster and a mansion. Gatsby's pathway to wealth and notoriety takes a different route than Meshach's, but their stories are quite similar in basic respects.

Gatsby's yachting cap seems a rather feeble item to be taken seriously as a symbol of such basic importance. Nick doesn't refer to it again in his narrative, but Fitzgerald does use the hat image importantly elsewhere in the book. On the title page there is a four-line verse written by "Thomas Parke D'Invilliers," alias Fitzgerald himself, that instructs a "gold-hatted, high-bouncing lover" how to win the woman he desires: "Then wear the gold hat, if that will move her;/ If you can bounce high, bounce for her too,/ Till she cry 'Lover, gold-hatted, high-bouncing lover,/ I must have you.'" I see here the influence on

Fitzgerald of *The Entailed Hat*. The behavior these lines enjoin, along with other similarities to features of *The Entailed Hat* that I discover in this novel, reassures me that Fitzgerald had GATH's book in mind as he was writing *The Great Gatsby*.

If the hats are symbols that reflect the influence of *Hat* on *Gatsby*, then some of the names in these two novels are also symbolic. For example, there is "Vesta," the name of Milburn's wife, and "Daisy," the name of Gatsby's beloved. In classical mythology, Vesta is goddess of the hearth, and her name evokes the virtues of purity and chastity. When we meet Vesta Custis, she is a child who pays Meshach the playful kindness one May day of tucking into his hatband a white rose, a flower that associates her with purity and innocence and beauty. In *The Great Gatsby*, Vesta's counterpart, Daisy, is a more ordinary, insubstantial, and short-lived flower. She is the "day's eye," radiant but temporal. Her maiden name, "Fay," suggests the blythe spirit of a fairy or nymph. The name "Myrtle" is also the name of a flower, one known for its showy red blooms—an appropriate name for the woman who is Tom Buchanan's brash mistress, a character who has no specific counterpart in *Hat*.

Townsend used names, we see, to enhance the symbolic value of some of his characters—including the name "Meshach," one of the three Biblical characters who escaped death in Nebuchadnezzar's fiery furnace. We should also note in this context that some critics interpret the name "Gatsby" as suggesting "God's Boy"—one favored by God. This name might also, and even simultaneously, suggest by its first three letters the slang term for a certain kind of pistol used by gangsters during the 1920's. I am tempted to see "GAT" as suggesting George Alfred Townsend's pen name "GATH": Jay, GATH's boy.[12]

Another similarity between *Gatsby* and *Hat* is that several of the prominent characters in both stories undergo a shift of identity. Meshach Milburn shifts social, economic, and character identity as he proceeds from his parents' cabin in the forest of Worcester County to his life as first a storekeeper, then as a money-lender, then as a member of the county's "first family," and finally as a self-appointed martyr for the county's welfare. His attitudes shift gradually, with the aid of Vesta's example. Other similar shifts occur as the novel proceeds: Vesta's father becomes less manipulative and more self controlled, Levin Dennis matures into a responsible adult, and Levin's father during his final hours of life repents of having deserted his family.

In Fitzgerald's novel, Nick Carraway, on the verge of committing himself to a career in brokerage and a set of Wall-Street values, details the story of Gatsby's rise to wealth and notoriety. In the novel that he writes when he returns home to the mid-west, Nick conveys the moral condition that materialism has nurtured during America's growth as a nation. Participating in this drama has threatened his personal identity in a frightening way. The values reflected in Nick's narrative are the 1925 equivalent of the material values portrayed by Townsend in *The Entailed Hat,* which reflects America a hundred years earlier. Wealth, position, and control are the key values of this system. The questions "who shall I become" and "how shall I proceed" affect Nick so that he has left New York and returned to the Middle-Western city where he was born, hoping to find there the idyll of his youth, or at least a fragment of it.

And so Nick becomes a sort of prophet, paralyzed into gasping "Beware!" To adopt Gatsby's solution to the dilemma of personal identity would be unnatural for Nick; luckily he refused it when Gatsby offered him the chance. But what is the alternative? Nick has similar problems with personal identity, and so does Jordan Baker, whom Nick might have married and then assumed a standard bland country-club persona. Jordan is faced with a similar issue. A woman, and one with only the most tenuous kind of material security, she needs to find a socially acceptable husband with money, or else settle for nonentity. If the designation "wife" does not constitute personal identity for her, it does at least guarantee her an acceptable role and save her from spinsterhood. In a sense, Jordan's dilemma is not so different from Myrtle Wilson's, though they are from an entirely different background socially. Both are women living in a culture where opportunity is a male prerogative. Each needs the support of a man to guarantee her financial security and to let her project the acceptable identity of "wife." Marrying Nick was Jordan's strategy for coming to terms with life, but Nick didn't cooperate. For Myrtle Wilson, a vulgar affair with Tom seemed to promise security. But we readers know that she was just a commodity, to be discarded after use.

The Entailed Hat includes no character who is quite like Jordan Baker. The closest candidate is Meshach's spirited niece, Rhoda Holland. Brought by Vesta to Princess Anne from the backwater farm where she was reared, Rhoda quickly becomes socially savvy and presentable. She is a spirited little character who soon receives a marriage proposal from the local Episcopal priest. Ultimately, though, she declines this offer and marries Vesta's father, Judge Custis, whose wife has divorced him and who is twice Rhoda's age. This may seem like opportunism on her part, and perhaps his, too. But both of them are clever, and her companionship stirs him to renewal of his spirit. Townsend's Rhoda and Fitzgerald's Jordan are alike in their desire to be married, but they are quite different in their attitude towards marriage. There is a good chance, I think, that Fitzgerald created Jordan as a negative foil to Rhoda, as Daisy is to Vesta.

The identity theme is also prominent in Townsend's depiction of Blacks and mulattos. Some of them are slaves with no choice but to do the bidding of their masters, and others (the "freedmen," for example) are little more privileged. This is something of a problem for Meshach, with his American Indian blood. He is not considered as a Black, but he is discriminated against as a half-breed. Those Blacks who have been freed are still, at best, objects of condescension. Especially, they live under the threat of being kidnapped and sold back into slavery. Persons in all these categories are disadvantaged by a social identity that compromises development of their natural talents and thwarts their personal advantage. There are also the poor, no matter what skin they wear—black, brown, or white. George and Myrtle Wilson are not "persons of color," but they are poor. The Wilsons live next to an enormous refuse dump outside New York City and depend for their subsistence on wealthy passers-by to buy from them the gasoline they need to power their expensive cars that take them where they want to go.

The social identity of such persons as these is very much to their disadvantage. In most cases, their lives are bound to be drab and unhappy. There are exceptions, however. Fitzgerald includes an example of this when he has Nick observe an instance of Blacks enjoying privileges usually reserved for wealthy Whites. As he rides with Gatsby in his elaborate Rolls-Royce over the Queensboro Bridge and onto Blackwell's Island, they are passed by a white-chauffeur-driven limousine. In the back "sat three modish Negroes, two bucks and a girl." Nick tells us that he laughed aloud "as the yolks of their eyeballs rolled towards us in haughty rivalry. 'Anything can happen now that we've slid over this bridge, anything at all,'" Nick thought, and adds, "'Even Gatsby could happen, without particular wonder'"(69). Here Nick seems strangely condescending. In fact, he seems nearly as bigoted as Tom Buchanan does in Chapter One when he champions the racial prejudice of a book called *The Rise of the Colored Empires* (13). For some groups of Americans, change of class identity is more difficult and remarkable than it is for others.

Similarly, Nick's account of his luncheon with Meyer Wolfsheim suggests he sympathizes with Tom's opinion that Jews are an upstart underclass that needs controlling. Nick's narrative presents Wolfsheim as a caricature straight out of vaudeville, complete with an accent, a "tragic nose," a ferocious appetite, and a focus on the dollar. However, Jews have developed a sense for "[seeing] the opportunity" that gives them advantage in the world of business. This, he implies, is fundamental to understanding their success (69-75). By his depiction of Wolfsheim Nick suggests he is a shade anti-Semitic. But on the other hand, he is narrating here an episode that happened during a time when his attitudes were maturing. Throughout the shifting present tense of the novel, Nick-the-narrator is a work in progress toward some ultimate Nick who is still developing, as Meshach Milburn develops in the course of *The Entailed Hat.*

An especially striking likeness between *Gatsby* and *Hat* is their prominent use of the image of the wasteland. This image figures prominently in the grail legend and harks back to at least the early Middle Ages in European literature, and to classical times in world literature. In the twentieth century T. S. Eliot gave it modern currency, focusing on the spiritual poverty of his own era. It is the same era that Fitzgerald depicts in *Gatsby*, and the same attitude. Fitzgerald's wasteland is the image of a vast acreage of ashes that he characterizes as a "fantastic farm where ashes grew like wheat" that is populated by "ashen gray men" who "move dimly and already crumbling through the powdery air." Past it flows a "small foul river" and through it pass railroad cars of ashen gray. Over it presides a decrepit billboard picturing two gigantic eyes that "brood on over the solemn dumping ground," eyes that George Wilson interprets as the eyes of God (23, 140). One of the most affecting images in twentieth-century American literature, it was inspired, quite possibly, by a similar extended image in *The Entailed Hat*.

In *Hat* Townsend presents a retouched description of an actual wasteland that existed in the area where he had lived for part of his childhood. Between Snow Hill and Princess Anne in Maryland's Worcester County, an industrial enterprise known as the Nassawongo Iron Furnace operated between

1829 and 1850. At this location, iron was extracted from the mud of a cypress bog in the forest and processed in a furnace fired with trees felled at the site. This process, which destroyed over a thousand square acres of trees per week to fuel the furnace and poisoned the air and groundwater in the area, yearly extracted about 700 tons of iron from the ore during the early years of its operation. Not only was the forest decimated, but the air was poisoned by sulfur fumes from the furnace, which burned night and day *(Fact Sheets)*.

Many of the workers and their families lived on the premises in company housing and earned a bare subsistence for their efforts. In the midst of this village was a large two-storey house used by the proprietor when he chose to be on site and by his deputy at other times. Meshach Milburn's family lived in this atmosphere during the last years of his parents' lives. When they died there of a fever, Meshach was left an orphan. Early in Townsend's novel, Meshach returns to the cabin that his family had occupied and bitterly sets it afire, symbolically severing identification with this part of his past.

Furnacetown was at least part of Fitzgerald's inspiration for the valley of ashes in *The Great Gatsby*, I believe. In the following description Townsend evokes an effect similar to the one Fitzgerald evokes in describing the ash-heap next to which George and Myrtle Wilson lived:

> [As] they entered the furnace village, . . . they saw the lights twinkle through the open doors of many cottages and the furnace flames darted over the forbidding mill-pond, where in the depths grew the iron ore like a vegetable creation, and above the surface, on splayed and conical mud-washed roots, the hundreds of strong cypresses towered from the water. . . . [The] furnace lake lay black and white and burning red as the shadows, or moonrise, or flames struck upon it. . . . Tawny, slimy, chilly, and solemn, the pond repeated the forms of the groves it submerged; the shaggy shadows added depth and dread to the effect; some strange birds hooted as they dipped their wings in the surface. (18-19)

Meshach, observing this scene of his boyhood, broods to himself, "'The earliest fools who turned up the bog ores for wealth . . . released the miasmas which slew all the people roundabout. They killed all my family, but set me free'" (19). Here Milburn curses the evils of the industrial/capitalistic ethic that has victimized his family. His name, Meshach, is appropriate to his character. The Biblical Meshach proved his faith by enduring the scorching flames of a fiery furnace and emerging alive, affirming to himself and the world the quality of his faith and the benison of his god. Townsend's Meshach requires help from an angel, his wife Vesta, to acquire the faith and goodness to which the final actions of his life attest.

In *Gatsby*, Myrtle Wilson, who lives at the edge of the valley of ashes with her broken, ashen husband, seeks something better for herself. What she finds with Tom is not savior from her lower-class misery but exploitation by him and death at being struck down by his carelessly driven sports car. We don't know the fate of the women in *Hat* who had affairs with Daniel Custis, owner of the Iron Furnace, and his foremen. We know only that a house-slave of his who had borne him a child met an unhappy end. Such persons as Tom Buchanan and the unreconstructed Judge Custis exploited men, women, and children of the lower classes, just as the wealthy and privileged still exploit their workers. Ironically, Custis, who went broke when the Furnace venture failed, had to sacrifice his daughter, Vesta, to marriage with Meshach in order to get money to pay his debts. In the course of the story, he gradually reforms, however, and works with Meshach on a project to benefit the public interest. Meanwhile, though, he has contributed to the malaise of American morale that Townsend and Fitzgerald depict.

In short, Townsend and Fitzgerald both dramatized the view that the American experiment in the course of its three centuries or so duration has gone frighteningly awry. The seeds of disappointment were planted by some of the earliest settlers in the seventeenth century, agents of commerce whose mission was to exploit the resources of the "new world" for the benefit of the clever and crafty. The hat that was entailed in the Milburn line was the hat of a criminal from England who allied himself with Dutch tradesmen in New York. In New York in the seventeenth century as elsewhere and at other times in the New World, personal freedom and equality of opportunity were features of the American ideal. But in America, concern with personal and corporate economics has dictated the national personality even more than in the mother countries that sent its first settlers across the Atlantic.

In the final paragraphs of *Gatsby*, Fitzgerald transforms the story of Jimmy Gatz from near-melodrama into epic by dramatizing Nick's perceptions of the Dutch sailors who first sailed up the Hudson. They had made their voyage in the name of commerce, but they were not insensitive to the beauty and promise of the new world, Nick suggests. Hitherto, Nick has represented the American Midwest, where he was reared, as a sort of Eden unspoiled by the commercialism he finds in New York. Here he can reflect on the course America has taken since the earliest days of colonization. Fitzgerald must have had a reason for choosing a Dutch sailor rather than an English sailor, or a Puritan, or a Catholic, or even a native American when he made this comparison. Probably it was because the Dutch are so closely identified with New York itself, the scene where the present-tense action is set. However, he may have chosen the Dutch rather than the English to further evoke the scenario of Meshach Milburn, whose ancestor seems to have been Dutch, or at least associated with Dutch trade in what then was New Amsterdam.

Assuming that Fitzgerald and Biggs did read *The Entailed Hat*, they were certainly struck by the concern with wealth and power that dominates the career of its protagonist. The "American Dream" as Townsend represents it is a lust for economic and personal control over others sufficient to guarantee an ambitious person comfort, security, personal freedom from want, and license to advance one's own personal benefit. Freedom to forge a personal identity that can exact this kind of control has been central to success in America from the earliest colonial times. However, behind the legal abstractions that guarantee and regulate this freedom is the spirit of competitive self-interest. The great extent to which this dynamic motivates personal and social behavior in America has caused Nick Carraway to retreat from it and seek a more humanistic environment.

Meshach Milburn, Jay Gatsby, and John Gault, the protagonist of John Biggs's *Demigods*, all aspire to power, wealth, and privilege. Through their efforts, all three of them achieve the symbols of superior status. They must maneuver cleverly to win from their adversaries the power and status they seek. The demands of this competition often conflict with basic ethical principles, so a certain hardness of heart is required in the player. To his credit, Nick Carraway does not qualify to play this game. Stunned by what he learns during his year in New York City, he returns to the comparative innocence of the small Midwest city where he was born. But seeing what he has seen of the broader world has paralyzed his will to engage further with modern life. As catharsis, he has written the novel about Gatsby.

The Entailed Hat and *Demigods*

Townsend and Fitzgerald both dramatized their view that the course of American history has run frighteningly awry. The seeds of disappointment were planted by some of the earliest settlers in the seventeenth century, agents of commerce whose mission was to exploit the resources of the "new world" to their own advantage. The hat that was entailed in the Milburn line was the hat of a man who had been jailed in England and eventually had allied himself with Dutch tradespersons in New York. In New York in the seventeenth century as elsewhere in frontier America, settlers had a divided allegiance: to the country that had sponsored their ventures, and to themselves, who had crossed an angry ocean and braved savages and fought with colonists from other countries attempting to gain personal advantage, quite possibly at the cost of their life. Their concern with self, and not with ideals, was most often their major concern, one must assume.

The mind-set of these colonists sets the note on which Fitzgerald concludes *The Great Gatsby*. He transforms the story of Jimmy Gatz from near-melodrama into epic when he alludes to the Dutch colonists who sailed up the Hudson River early in America's recent past. They had made their voyage in the name of commerce, but they were not insensitive to the beauty and promise of the new world, Nick suggests in his book's final paragraphs. For most, however, self-interest was the motive, and from that they could not be long distracted. Like Meshach and Gatsby, Nick was in New York with the object of making a career for himself. But unlike them he had values that money and status alone would not satisfy. After the Gatsby affair he retreated back to his hometown in the Midwest, expecting to find in force there the values that had been all but rejected in such worldly centers as New York.

The human animal is not content just "to have" but must have yet more and more. This theme is at the center of *The Entailed Hat* and *The Great Gatsby,* and also at the core of *Demigods.* Biggs, like Fitzgerald, implied his debt to George Alfred Townsend by dramatizing in his novel the theme of aspiration, as Fitzgerald also does.[13] In addition, Biggs gave his protagonist a name that evokes Townsend's pen-name by using three of its four letters in his protagonist's name. The initials are "G," "A," and "T," as in *Gatsby* and *Gath*, and the character is John *Gault*.[14] This identification does not stop with the name. Biggs also gave John Gault certain traits and experiences of George Alfred Townsend himself. Finally, these three novels—*Demigods*, *Gatsby*, and *Hat*—and their protagonists bear essential likenesses to one another. To see them, we need to establish the plot line and essential features of *Demigods*, which, like *The Entailed Hat*, is not well known to present-day readers.

In *Demigods* the career of John Gault and essentials of the career of his father, Hosea Gault, are related by an anonymous third-person narrator writing this account in 1922. He proceeds chronologically, first reviewing the career of Hosea Gault, whom he apostrophizes as a man of "burning vitality" and "vast restlessness," "a man aflame," the prophet of "a god of dreams and visions." But, he tells us, "this history concerns itself with the son," who must be seen in the light of his father (Biggs 3-9). This characterization reminds us of how Fitzgerald depicts Gatsby as a "son of God" who "must be about his Father's business, the service of a vast, vulgar, and meretricious beauty" (99).

Hosea Gault is a fiercely fanatic religionist, a Dunkard who in the mid-nineteenth century led a group of fundamentalist Christians on a three-year trek seeking a place to locate a community exclusively their own. This effort recalls the Puritans, who sailed to the New World to establish a New Jerusalem, and also, perhaps, the Mormons who followed Joseph Smith from New York to Ohio in the nineteenth century. Hosea feels driven by divine inspiration in this task, but at times he suspects he might merely be serving himself rather than serving the purpose of God. Biggs's narrator underscores Hosea's self-doubt when he tells us, "Gault did not know what purpose his god was making manifest to him. He did not care to inquire. . . . [I]t seemed to him that he was designated to be the prophet of a new and pure religion, which should arise by his hands out of a wilderness" (6). There is no character in *The Great Gatsby* like Hosea Gault, and the Episcopal priest in *The Entailed Hat* was more pious than zealous. However, there were the Puritan leaders of similar zeal who led colonists to New England in the seventeenth century. It is the influence of this particular consort of American settlers that John Biggs traces through his protagonist, John Gault.

Like Gatsby and Meshach, Hosea Gault is a monomaniac driven to exalt himself to prominence and leadership. More to the point, he is, or at least fancies himself to be, a demigod, a human being of superior potential whom the gods have ordained to promote their agenda. Such persons are born divinely equipped to perform a god-given role, according to the belief system of this sect. However, they retain the power of personal will, a power that might cause them to pursue a personal agenda of their own, one that possibly differs from the role they have been programmed for. Hosea Gault has boldly and aggressively accepted his role as a missionary of the gods, but his son, John Gault, rebels against becoming his father's successor. Instead, he spends his life trying to fashion an identity he contrives on his own. In the language of Biggs's cryptic introduction to the book, Hosea's son John was a "Charlatan." As the story progresses, we come to see a Charlatan as a person who chooses a different course in life than the one the gods intended him to pursue. He feels his way towards fulfillment by following values of his own and working toward goals that are constantly changing.

Possibly John Biggs drew the defining elements of his plot from some source or other. But I suspect it includes a touch of autobiography, that he used John Gault to represent an identity dilemma that he knew or could imagine. Biggs's father and grandfather were respectively governor and attorney general of Delaware, and John Biggs, Jr., was preparing for a similar career by studying law. But at Princeton he quite probably had second thoughts and decided that his own special talent was writing. During the 1920's he published two novels and some short stories, and he seems to have written one or two other novels that were not published. This choice between identities, between the life he seems to have been born to live and the life he attempted to live, is a central theme in *Demigods*. Here again we see the personal identity theme in action, as it is in *The Entailed Hat* and *The Great Gatsby*. If so, Biggs gave the theme a distinctly personal significance.

From the time he was a young child, John Gault resisted succeeding his father as spiritual and civic leader of Boontown, the community that Hosea and his followers established in New Hampshire after three years of wandering. Orphaned by his father before he was born, John willfully resisted the creed and discipline of the Dunkards and sought out for guidance an uncle of his, his mother's brother. John's mother, Aurora Merton, and her alcoholic brother, Gil, had come into the community by chance: Hosea Gault had rescued them from drowning during a flood of the Israel River, which flowed past the Dunkard settlement. Hosea had married Aurora soon thereafter and died before their son, John, was born. By the time he was in his early teens, John Gault had had enough of Boontown. He was considered heir-apparent to his father, but from his very infancy he aggressively resisted preparing for his role as leader of the Dunkard community. After he attacked and possibly killed a man at age thirteen, he fled east across the mountains of New Hampshire's Presidential Range, determined never to return.

Thenceforth the narrator of *Demigods* chronicles John Gault's career, first in Philadelphia, where he was tossed overboard from a boat on which he had stowed away, and later in Delaware, where he worked at creating an adult identity that suited him—several consecutive identities, in fact. His figurative baptism by immersion, a prominent article of Dunkard theology, occurs symbolically several times in the course of *Demigods*. In contrast, when the rebellious John Gault dies, he dies by fire. Literally from the waters of the Delaware River Gault emerged homeless and penniless in Philadelphia and got his first glimpse of the gaudy world of gilded-age East-Coast America. In every way it was the antithesis of Boontown. This was a late-nineteenth-century version of the world that Gatsby saw and aspired to triumph in, and a microcosm of the world of high finance that Meshach qualified himself to enter.

After walking the streets wide-eyed and amazed, John Gault met a man who became his second mentor. Meshach Milburn, in *Hat*, is mentored by the spirit of his ancestor Jacob Milbourne, and Gatsby learned about life from the rare-metals prospector Dan Cody. Gault was educated to adult life in the larger world by a withered old skeptic who was living in poverty in the loft of an old warehouse when they met. He had been born to a wealthy family named Deroulet but had re-invented himself and re-named himself Christopher Herrick. Herrick recognized genius in John Gault and with open cynicism educated this grotesque, strapping, red-faced young genius haphazardly about life, literature, and the ways of the world. He knew that Gault "was born under the charlatan's star which permits no ease" and intuited that "the perpetual madness of his soul [would impel] him towards ends of which he was unaware" (78).

Eventually Herrick warned Gault mysteriously, "'Your land is not here. . . . It is beyond the horizon of a dream, but you may win to it before you are consumed at your certain end'" (113). Before he died, Herrick spoke a monologue to John Gault that epitomizes a central theme of this novel and of Townsend's and Fitzgerald's, too: the search for personal identity. He tells Gault,

> "I know you well, know your swift, intractable spirit, your pride. . . . Civilization, the traditions of mankind, are not for you. *You must find a people and a barren land, lead hosts to a newer heaven as did your father.* . . . Do not struggle with the devices and tricks of man. Reject them! Do not place yourself upon the world. You will betray yourself, prove false to the godhead that is in you. . . . . You will be as incapable of escaping your destiny as I have been in escaping mine. You will grow great, pass, and terribly die. . . . The real futility is that one is bound, that one can render so little of oneself. . . . Ride your life, John Gault! . . . I have never been able to ride mine!"
> (154-55; Biggs's italics)

Predestination, as Biggs's narrator has presented it in speaking of Hosea Gault's mania, is a mystical, incontrovertible force. It is not a matter merely of social or biological conditioning or of reaction against conditioning that one has been subjected to. It is a divinely ordained "given." Meshach Milburn may or may not have been predestined to become an orphan, recover his ancestral hat, marry Vesta, and ride his financial success to the benefit of his community. GATH does not plunge so deeply into metaphysics. Gatsby, on the other hand, is perceived by Nick Carraway as "a Platonic conception," a "son of God" who "must be about his Father's business, the service of a vast, vulgar, and meretricious beauty" (99). John Gault, too, is such a person: one who is ruled by cosmic forces beyond his control, who must "ride" the life the gods have committed him to. The alternative, Herrick warns, is to betray himself, to "'prove false to the godhead that is in [him].'" His advice is to "'Ride your life, John Gault!'" (154-55). Gault does not do this; he continues resisting the will of the gods until the very last phase of his life, by which time the gods had despaired of him and thought only to punish him by treating him as a failure. If we interpret Gatsby's career in these terms, we might conclude (1) that he did "ride the life" ordained for him by the gods, and not question why they ordained such a life for him, and possibly also conclude (2) that Gatsby's values arose from some other source or mechanism.

In counterpoise to John Gault is his co-worker Acie Carrol, a tall, thin, pallid young man who knew neither his parents nor when he was born. Biggs depicts him paradoxically as devoted to the building of ships but frightened of the water and hating the ships he has helped build the moment they are launched. The two explored Philadelphia together, soon becoming fast friends. From a fortune teller, they discovered the nature of their fate. Carrol was told that his death would involve "a rope of cold, cruel hemp." And so it did: after nearly being killed in a mishap at the shipyard, he killed the man who caused the accident and, we are left to believe, was punished by hanging (159-65).

Gault's own destiny was more vague. The fortune teller looked at his palm and enigmatically echoed Herrick's admonition to "ride his life." "A horse which you may ride" is what she saw in his future. After winning enormously at dice later that evening, Gault assumed she meant his fortune was in his own hands, "his red fists" with which "he smashed . . . whatever . . . stood before him" (146-47). This affirms what John Gault has already declared to Herrick: "'If I shall be destroyed . . . it shall be by action indomitably my own'" (138). Chapters four and five dramatize John Gault's attempt to achieve a destiny of his own choosing through means of his own choice. Gatsby does this by becoming a criminal and pursuing Daisy. Meshach does it by winning Vesta and by becoming a shady financial broker, to the ruin of his health.

In August, 1890, bereft of his friends Herrick and Carrol, Gault ventured down the Delaware River to Wilmington possessed by a vision. In a daze of impulse, he wildly roamed the streets seeking recruits to follow him towards realizing a twisted destiny that even he could not define. Obviously he was feeling the pull of the destiny his father had accepted but that he himself had resisted. In the wild imagination of John Gault, however, it gave him the task of "growing men" in the Delaware countryside "by sowing salt in the furrows of the earth" (168). This dream summons to mind the iron-furnace landscape of *The Entailed Hat* and Fitzgerald's valley of ashes: the wasteland image. The gods seemed still to be exhorting him to his predestined task.

For wildly ranting about this dream on a Wilmington street corner, Gault was arrested and sentenced to labor for a month on a barren farm—yet another injunction of the gods to be the savior/hero he was intended to become. Then, after thieving for a while and toiling at various menial jobs, Gault had the luck to buy a bankrupt printing business at public auction and—rather like Meshach Milburn in *Hat*—became a successful businessman within a few years. Still not satisfied, he studied law and entered practice, but his high-pitched voice, unnaturally red complexion, and grotesque obesity made him such a laughingstock that he left law and returned to publishing. Still he considered himself an independent agent in designing his life.

John Gault grew stouter and redder as his newspapers made him more and more wealthy and his success made him more vain. At length he convinced himself he could become Governor of Delaware and marry the wealthiest and most beautiful woman in the state. His control of the state's newspapers would guarantee him political success, he felt, and the country estate he bought would help him win the woman he wanted. His hopes were high, but his efforts were doomed to failure. His haughty socialite lady friend rejected him brutally with a public display of contempt—even more brutally than Daisy rejected Gatsby—and he lost the election by an embarrassing margin.

Humiliated, Gault abandoned the life he had made for himself and disappeared in the middle of the night. The book's narrator reveals to us his fate. In despair of finding a satisfactory life for himself, he surrendered finally to the calling the gods had intended for him: evangelist to the poor people who occupied a squalid setting that recalls Townsend's Furnacetown and Fitzgerald's Ash Heaps. Ironically, by this time the gods seem to have abandoned him as their agent. His every attempt was failure. Finally, Gault died a terrible death by entering a fiery furnace with two fellow religionists, playing Meshach to their Shadrach and Abednego. Whatever he might have expected, he was not saved by faith from a fiery death. The narrator, whose heroic prose style conveys his fascination with Gault's career, concludes emotionally in these final paragraphs that "John Gault, still searching, had not found his world" (227).

Observations and Conclusions

In John Gault's story, as in Meshach Milburn's and Jay Gatsby's, the American way of regarding human nature and regulating human interchange is depicted and challenged. Material values are the guideposts of American ambition, and commerce is the means of fulfilling it. Given basic human greed, which causes man to seek the ultimate of security and comfort, and considering the competitive nature of the human animal, a democratic society must encourage mutual consideration among its citizens. Apparently Biggs and Fitzgerald recognized the cogency of Townsend's critique and sought to revive it for their own generation. As in Gath's "historical romance," Biggs's novel and Fitzgerald's novel both focus on a disadvantaged young person facing the future offered him by contemporary America. It is a place where personal advantage is gained only through moral callousness.

With his religious background, intellectual training, and experience as a journalist, George Alfred Townsend was well equipped in his forties to write *The Entailed Hat*. In their twenties, Biggs and Fitzgerald were less experienced with life at the extremes of the social spectrum but were ripe to be instructed by Townsend. The figure that John Gault cuts in the last two chapters of *Demigods* actually suggests Gath physically and dramatically. Gath and John Gault both were sons of a fundamentalist minister. Both were journalists, and both practiced law. Gault, like Gath, was a large, heavy man with a red complexion, and like young Townsend, John Gault had an ineffective speaking voice (Townsend's delivery improved as he got older). Also both Gath and Gault had a significant pre-marital relationship with a European woman, and both were deserted by their lover. Both of these men afterward proposed marriage to a woman of superior social status, Gath actually marrying his lady, while John Gault and Jay Gatsby were turned down by theirs. John Biggs, Jr., may have also worked some of his own autobiography into *Demigods*, as I have suggested above, and his John Gault practiced law for a while, which Biggs did after attending Harvard Law School and prior to becoming a judge. It has been suggested that Biggs's family and the Townsend family might actually have known each other when they both lived in the area of Delaware City. This family tradition may have helped inspire Biggs to write *Demigods*.

Whatever the inspiration might have been, the fact is obviously this: that these three novels are similar sufficiently that they merit comparison. Speculation logically leads me to believe that *The Entailed Hat* influenced the writing of both *Demigods* and *The Great Gatsby*. All three books present a critique of American materialism; all three of them feature a self-absorbed protagonist whose ambition leads him to fashion a life for himself different from the one he seemed destined to pursue; and the three novels use similar symbols, situations, and characters to create their effect. Each writer employs a style of his own and conveys a slightly different attitude towards his themes and the characters he uses to present them. In their execution, these three works are very individual but are also much alike.

One remembers *The Entailed Hat* for its historical local color and its treatment of the slavery issue and possibly its touch of romantic melodrama. *Demigods* has a larger-than-life mythicism about it that makes it distinctive, and *Gatsby* has its jazz-age atmosphere and its Conradian narrator and narrative structure among other features that have lodged it in the canon of twentieth-century American fiction. But as individual as they may be in personality, these three books are significantly like each other thematically.

It seems logical, then, to say that George Alfred Townsend's *The Entailed Hat* strongly influenced both Biggs and Fitzgerald in portraying the American experience for their own generation. One dominant theme of all three works is personal ambition: the compulsion of a bright, clever young man to transcend his origins and achieve superior influence in and beyond his community. This ambition leads all three protagonists to develop a distinctive personal identity and not just play out a set of roles dictated by fate. Meshach, John Gault, and Gatsby have all three taken circumstances in hand and crafted themselves into strong, interesting, compelling individuals. They have felt their way impulsively past obstacles and satisfied their basic human compulsion for control of both themselves and others. Idealism, spirituality, and social concern are factors in the formation of their character, often in a warped or twisted way; but self concern is the notable factor in the life of all three protagonists.

In unfolding their protagonists' search for means to forge success for themselves in American society, Townsend, Fitzgerald, and Biggs are above all else critiquing the American experience. The depiction by Fitzgerald and Biggs of New York and Philadelphia as meccas of self-gratification, and suggestions dropped by Townsend about the mercenary atmosphere of Baltimore, suggest wasteland scapes that portray the shady underside of America's promise. All three of these writers are concerned about the course of America's development. Writing in the 1880's, Townsend looked back on slavery and industrial servitude, inviting his readers to analyze the current scene in terms of the past that produced it. Fitzgerald and Biggs similarly address their readership in the twenties.

A difference between Townsend's treatment of these themes and the treatment given them by Biggs and Fitzgerald is Townsend's more baldly melodramatic approach to his material. The use by both Biggs and Fitzgerald of a Conradian first-person narrator corrected this problem by minimizing the air of moral preachment and thus requiring critical involvement from the reader. In addition, Fitzgerald seems to have been challenged by Townsend's voluminous plot to achieve the stylistic economy that

Gatsby is known for. Like Fitzgerald, Biggs reduces Townsend's disjointed narrative to less than half the length, developing the same problems of personal and national identity through the mythic sensibility of an observer who is deeply and personally engaged in the story he is telling. The effect of both comes across as more dramatic than didactic.

Though *Gatsby* and *Hat* correspond with each other in a number of ways, there is no mention of Townsend or allusion to *The Entailed Hat* anywhere in the letters between Fitzgerald and Biggs or Fitzgerald and Maxwell Perkins that I have read. And there is no mention of *Demigods* by title in the published correspondence; *Seven Days Whipping* is the only one of the novels and short stories that Biggs produced that is mentioned by name. A letter written by Fitzgerald to Biggs in the spring of 1939 might suggest why this is so. "Someday," he says in the letter, "I'm going to write about the great difference between how you high-heartedly helped me get over a hurdle and the heartburnings and humiliations that I went thru [sic] in the process of approaching you." Conscious that his letters would survive him, he has explained a few lines earlier that he is "now writing this letter for my files as well as to you" (Turnbull 604-05). Undoubtedly Biggs had done Fitzgerald many favors, some of them financial, possibly, and some of them personal, to be sure. But the one alluded to here seems to have been very special, one that Fitzgerald is not ready yet, in 1939, to detail in letters or files that were destined to be made public. Might it have had to do with *Gatsby* and *Demigods* and *Hat*?

In this letter he follows the habit he had of recommending—and passing critical judgment on—books he had recently read. Writing from California, where he was trying to produce scripts for the movies, he recommends Kafka's *The Trial* and especially Malraux's *Man's Fate*, grim works that question the efficacy of human will (Turnbull 605). This is a theme that would be of interest to the author of *Demigods*, to be sure. Exchanges like this, which occurred at Princeton among the literary set of Fitzgerald's years there, most likely led Fitzgerald to read and appreciate *The Entailed Hat*, if he had not read it already. So, it was quite possible that it was Biggs who put him onto it, or reminded him of it, in 1924 and not, for example, Edmund Wilson. Wilson praised *Gatsby* highly, but he was severe in criticizing Fitzgerald's earlier work (Kazin 77). If Wilson had noticed Fitzgerald's debt to Townsend, he certainly would have mentioned it in writing about *Gatsby*.

In the 1939 letter to Biggs, Fitzgerald also addresses the issue that is Biggs's main concern in *Demigods*: adult identity. "I hope you'll be a better judge than I've been a man of letters," Fitzgerald says to this man who had once shared his ambition to become a professional writer and recently had become the youngest judge of the U.S. Circuit Court of Appeals ever to have been appointed (Turnbull 605; Meyers 24).

Some Implications and Further Conclusions

It seems clear to me that these three novels are sufficiently similar that they merit comparison and invite speculation concerning the influence of *The Entailed Hat* on the other two. Surprisingly, Maxwell Perkins, who was Scribner's editor of both *Demigods* and *Gatsby*, did not see correspondence between these two novels or between them and *Hat*, or possibly did see it and let it pass. Also remarkable is the amount and degree of "self-puffery" that exists in Fitzgerald's letters to Perkins during the time he was writing *Gatsby*. I believe that Perkins's good opinion was so important to Fitzgerald that he did not even hint to his editor that *Gatsby* was influenced by either Biggs or Townsend. Interesting in this context is the paragraph that he wrote to Perkins about fellow writer Arthur Train while he himself was writing *Gatsby:* "I enjoyed Arthur Train's story in the *Post* but he made three steals on the first page—one from Shaw, one from Standahl [sic], and one I've forgotten. It was most ingeniously worked out—I never could have handled such an intricate plot in a thousand years" (Turnbull 184). This is an interesting insight into Fitzgerald's mind-set at the time.

Whether or not one accepts all of these premises, *Gatsby* and *Demigods* need to be considered in terms of "borrowing" or at least of "influence." All three books—*Gatsby, Demigods,* and *Hat*—present a critique of America's materialistic values; all three of them feature a self-absorbed protagonist whose ambition leads him to fashion a life for himself different from the one he seemed destined to pursue; and the three of them use similar symbols, situations, and characters to create their effect. Each writer employs a style of his own and dramatizes his themes with a different emphasis. But these three works are significantly similar to each other thematically and in some respects stylistically, as we have seen.

When and how Fitzgerald encountered *The Entailed Hat* is a matter of conjecture, as we have noted. It seems logical to assume he knew of this work before he met Biggs, or that possibly Biggs introduced him to it while they were at Princeton together. It might also be that the manuscript by Biggs that Fitzgerald, in February, 1920, asked H. L. Mencken to read, was the work that Scribner published later, in 1926, as *Demigods*. If this was the case, by the time Fitzgerald wrote *Gatsby*, he would have had several years' acquaintance with Townsend's book, and through it, with *The Entailed Hat*.

Or it might be that Biggs intended the narrator of *Demigods* to invoke Biggs himself when the narrator says, "Granary Ground *upon this day in June, 1922*, has changed but little from the form which was set upon it by Hosea Gault" (28, italics mine). The lines refer to the burial place of Gault, the elder, who died when he challenged God, commanding Him to calm flood waters that were overwhelming the community Gault had founded (46-49). The narrator of *Demigods* is so impressed by the Gault saga that he has made a pilgrimage to the site where Boontown once existed and discovered there are no traces of it remaining. If this passage was indeed written in 1922, it coincides with the period of Biggs's life when he had to decide whether to challenge what seems to have been God's will for his own destiny—i.e., to continue at Harvard preparing for a career in law, or to make a career of writing. Seen thus, Biggs might convincingly have been an inspiration for Nick Carraway, who is poised between an unrepeatable past and a possibly unsatisfying future.

If this was the case, Fitzgerald knew both *The Entailed Hat* and the essentials of *Demigods* and had them available as influences when he was writing *Gatsby* in 1924. Biggs's writing style is quite different from Fitzgerald's; Maxwell Perkins characterized his early style as "fantastic . . . [with an] almost insane imaginative quality" (Bruccoli and Duggan 233). The plot, technique, and verbal style of Biggs and Fitzgerald are very individual, but both novels do employ a number of Townsend's themes and character types and also, it should be noted, a Conradian first-person narrator.

We notice these correspondences and recall that Fitzgerald was having problems writing his third novel until sometime in the spring of 1924, when he shifted from a false start he had made to a fresh inspiration that rapidly produced *The Great Gatsby*. Perhaps it was then, or maybe it was even earlier, that he picked up raw material that led him to the "Dutch sailors" allusion he placed on the last page, universalizing the effect of Nick's narrative (Johnson 113-15). This depiction of America as an Eden subject to corruption by European greed uses Dutch sailors, and not English or French or Spanish sailors. "Why?" we might ask. Certainly because New York, by 1924 the epitome of American modernism, was once New Amsterdam—and prior to that was virgin forest. And it might also have been that Fitzgerald had been reading about Meshach Milburn's entailed hat.

As Fitzgerald's critics and fellow writers noticed early in his career, his writing does show the influence of other novelists. Arthur Mizener remarks that Fitzgerald "was never very conscious of his literary debts" (186). But many other critics have made a good case that he was more conscious of them than Mizener's remark suggests. For example, Nancy Milford in her biography of Fitzgerald's wife holds that he used portions of Zelda's diary in "The Jelly Bean" and that he "had drawn on some of her . . . writing in *This Side of Paradise.*"[15] Other critics, too, have remarked on Fitzgerald's habit of borrowing, and Fitzgerald himself was aware of the influences he noticed in the works of fellow writers. In 1926 Gilbert Seldes called *This Side of Paradise* "a stepchild of [Compton Mackenzie's] *Sinister Street,*" a comparison made by Edmund Wilson, as well. Seldes also observed in it traces of H. G. Wells, and remarked that *The Beautiful and Damned* and *Gatsby* both show the influence of Edith Wharton and Joseph Conrad. In *Gatsby* he observed, too, the influence of Henry James, but felt that "Fitzgerald has at last made his borrowings his own" (Seldes 125-26).

Critic Robert Roulston has devoted a sizable article to summarizing opinions about Fitzgerald's borrowings in *The Great Gatsby*. He prefaces this roundup by generalizing that "a catalog of the authors whose writings have supposedly left traces on *The Great Gatsby* is as full of bizarre incongruities as Nick Carraway's list of guests at Gatsby's parties" and includes Stephen Leacock, Charles Dickens, Ford Maddox Ford, Petronius, Stendhal, and Oswald Spengler among the many whose work influenced Fitzgerald to one degree or another (54). But Roulston concludes that *Gatsby* is not a hodgepodge of borrowings from any one or several philosophers or writers but a cleverly integrated work that projects unity and genius (Donaldson 63).

Edmund Wilson, one of the critics who knew Fitzgerald best, criticized his lack of depth. In fact, by the time Fitzgerald was working on his third novel, Wilson, who knew Fitzgerald and his work from their days at Princeton, wrote that

Fitzgerald "had a gift of expression without many ideas to express," and opines that "he is not much given to abstract or impersonal thought" and is too greatly "wrapped up in his dream of himself and his projection of it on paper" (Kazin 82-84). During the spring of 1924, while he was working on the novel that would become *The Great Gatsby*, Fitzgerald criticized himself for having "deteriorated in the three years since I finished *The Beautiful and Damned*." In writing his new novel, he says, he was "thrown directly on purely creative work—not trashy imaginings as in my stories but the sustained imagination of a sincere yet radiant world. . . . This book will be a consciously artistic achievement and must depend on that as the first books did not" (Turnbull 182-83). On its publication, Wilson enthused in a letter to Hamilton Basso that he found it vivid and exciting, well planned, well sustained, and excitingly, dramatically written (Meyers 129). Maxwell Perkins's letter to Fitzgerald about *Gatsby* is as complimentary as Fitzgerald might possibly have wished: "The manuscript is full of phrases which made a scene blaze with life. . . . You have plainly mastered the craft . . . but you needed far more than craftsmanship for this" (Donaldson 262).

Fitzgerald himself had declared to Perkins, "I think that at last I've done something really my own" (Turnbull 188). If he did indeed borrow from Townsend and/or Biggs and possibly others, is this self-praise any less valid? However much there is in *Gatsby* of Townsend or Biggs, Fitzgerald had achieved what a novelist hopes to achieve: production of a dramatic, well-crafted, profound, effective work of art. To the extent that he shows a talent for organizing and presenting a complex of themes subtly and effectively, he has worked in the tradition of Shakespeare, another great borrower. If Fitzgerald worked with themes, characters, and situations suggested to him by *The Entailed Hat*, as I think he and Biggs both did, they first worked backward toward essences and then forward in re-embodying them. This explains much, I think, about why *Gatsby* was so much deeper in content and richer in style than his previous novels. He had themes and the outline of a plot securely in mind as he wrote, and was thus able to concentrate on what he did best: dramatizing and organizing the action, bringing his characters to life, and expressing the whole in fine, tight prose.

Whether Fitzgerald was actually inspired by Townsend's novel, and whether he and Biggs discussed it together, I can only speculate about on the basis of such circumstantial and textual evidence as I have presented. His letters to Perkins make it clear, though, that he was desperate to develop a novel that would establish him as a serious-minded writer whom critics would praise and whose public would buy his book in great numbers. Early in 1924, before he had finished writing *Gatsby*, he wrote to Perkins that he had just about used up his fund of personal experience, and that he had "talked so much and not lived enough within myself to develop . . . self-reliance. . . . This book will be a conscientiously artistic achievement and must depend on that as the first books did not" (Turnbull 183).

By then he had decided against using in this new novel the plot and characters that figured later in the short story "Absolution." By August 27, 1924, he was confident enough to suggest that the new novel would be finished in early September (Turnbull 185). What happened during the preceding half-year to set Fitzgerald on course we can only speculate about. I suggest it was something related to reflecting on the text of *The Entailed Hat* and "talking ideas" with Biggs. His novel projected the contemporary atmosphere that readers expected from Fitzgerald, but importantly, it dramatized themes that marked the work as "serious" and gave it significance beyond the immediate personal and social scene. Above all, it accomplished its purpose with serious intent and in signature style.

In my opinion, then, Fitzgerald's acquaintance with *The Entailed Hat* gave him the parameters of a plot and the seed of several important themes. The telling genius of *The Great Gatsby* is Fitzgerald's integration of these elements into a dynamic, meaningful drama that reflects the American scene in which he and his readers were living in 1925. To give his story historical resonance, he cleverly projected a theme of contemporary importance by having Gatsby—and Nick, himself—stubbornly resist the truth that inevitably time brings change. It is a novel about Fitzgerald's own milieu, but it is also a study of human nature, and the nature of American values, and indeed the nature of history. It is the sort of study that every generation of every human culture needs in assessing where it has arrived in the course of passing time. I am by no means challenging its worthiness of praise. In fact, I think it is especially valuable as a national critique because it projects so many elements of Townsend's own national critique over the intervening hundred years between the 1820's and the 1920's, and is no less valid today.

Reading and pondering *The Entailed Hat* and, I assume, discussing it with John Biggs gave him perspective and inspired him artistically, I think. With a set of ideas in mind and a master plan of his own contrivance, he was free to devote his wit and cleverness to doing the things he did best: telling a story dramatically, elegantly, and economically. Fitzgerald's knowing *The Entailed Hat* was a great help in releasing the talent that made this novel really great.

NOTES

[1] See Bruccoli and Duggan, footnote 312. Bruccoli says that Key was not Fitzgerald's great-grand-uncle as some authorities claim he was, but instead was his second cousin three times removed. In a manuscript written near the end of his life, Townsend mentions Francis Scott Key, "the lawyer bard," as a brother-in-law of Chief Justice Roger Brooke Taney, whose "Dred Scott Decision" Townsend found execrable. Francis Scott Key and Taney were also partners in a law practice they launched in 1801 in Frederick, Maryland.

Shields tells us in his biography of Townsend that F. S. Key's uncle Philip Barton Key was a commissioned officer in the British Army during the American Revolution. In 1778 P. B. Key shifted sides and soon thereafter was taken prisoner by the British while he was serving as a captain in the Continental Army. Paroled by the British, he went to England, but in 1785 he returned to Maryland to practice law and in 1807 was elected as a Maryland representative to the U.S. Congress (Shields 81).

[2] In a letter to me, John Biggs III suggests interestingly that his own family and the family of Reverend Stephen Townsend might have known each other: "Gath was born in Georgetown [Delaware] and lived variously on the Delmarva Peninsula until he graduated in 1860 in Philadelphia. My grandfather was born in Middletown

and his grandfather at Duck Creek, now Smyrna. Thus there should have been an overlap of families certainly in the 1820's" (November 8, 2003).

[3] "Delmarva" refers to the peninsula on which the state of Delaware, nine counties of Maryland, and two counties of Virginia are located. It is bordered on the east by the Atlantic Ocean and on the west by the Chesapeake Bay, which meet at the south end of the peninsula. The Maryland portion of this lengthy finger of land is known as "the Eastern Shore of Maryland," or simply "the Eastern Shore."

[4] Townsend's parents were both born on the Eastern Shore. George Alfred Townsend's father became successively a carpenter, an itinerant Methodist preacher, and a doctor. Mrs. Townsend was born Mary Milborn in Maryland's Worcester or Somerset County, of "Eastern Shore stock" (Brewington, vii, in "Foreword" to *The Entailed Hat*).

[5] The last mention I have seen of John Biggs, Jr., as a writer is in a letter from Fitzgerald to Maxwell Perkins; in it, he requests "news of the play" by John Biggs. Fitzgerald was writing in June, 1929, from France.

[6] Some critics have written that Fitzgerald and Biggs were roommates at Princeton. John Biggs III questions whether Fitzgerald and his father were actually roommates except for a brief period after Fitzgerald was rusticated

in 1917, when the two of them were completing one or more writing projects they had begun together as student editors of certain Princeton publications. Otherwise, Biggs "roomed in Campbell and Fitzgerald in Patton" (Biggs III, 1).

Fitzgerald was most likely using the term metaphorically when in a letter he wrote to Edmund Wilson during the fall of 1917 he referred to Biggs as "my roommate" (Turnbull 343) . The labors they shared in editing and writing for *The Tiger* and *The Nassau Lit* must have required them to spend a lot of time together. "Biggs and I do the prose [for the *Lit*]—Creese and Keller . . . and I [do] the poetry," the letter says (Turnbull 343-44) .

[7] Biggs wrote a novel earlier, the manuscript of which Fitzgerald sent to H. L. Mencken in February, 1920, for an opinion. It had been rejected by Scribner and by Putnam "on the grounds of obscurity," Fitzgerald explained to Mencken. In his cover letter, Fitzgerald praises the manuscript as having "the most beautiful writing—and I don't mean 'fine' writing—that I've seen in a 'coon's age" (Bruccoli and Duggan 78). This may—or may not—have been a draft of *Demigods*. A letter from Perkins to Fitzgerald dated November 20, 1929, reveals that Biggs wrote at least one more novel, one that Perkins declined to publish because "it did not seem to have the life and power of his others; and besides he had been Hemingway'd. . . . [O]ne would not expect it of

so marked an individual as John" (Bruccoli and Duggan 233). It would seem that Biggs wrote a total of three and perhaps four or more novels, at least one play (Turnbull 238, 240), and some short stories.

[8] In his introduction to *Hat*, Townsend alludes to *The Scarlet Letter* specifically, and the drama in the final pages of *Hat* suggests he was inspired by "The Minister's Black Veil." Another notably Hawthornean passage occurs in Chapter Five when Milburn broods over his past as he prepares to set fire to the cabin where his family once lived (28-31).

[9] The original text, with illustrations and a foreword by M. V. Brewington, was reprinted in 1955 and at least once thereafter by Tidewater Publishers of Cambridge MD. In addition, the book appeared in a version published in 2000 by Nanticoke Books of Vienna MD, edited by Hal Roth. Readers should know that in this later edition, Roth has adjusted Gath's text to make the book "more acceptable to the modern reader" by "modifying spelling, punctuation, and often the structure of sentences and paragraphs to hopefully make them more appealing and smooth flowing," he says on page three of his foreword. *George Alfred Townsend*, by Ruthanna Hindes (Hambleton Printing and Publishing Co., 1946), and the essay by Jerry Shields, "A Sketch of His Life," in *Gath's Literary Work and Folk*, provide valuable biographical detail about Townsend. Shields also published the article

"What Hath 'Gath' Wrought?" in *Collecting Delaware Books*, 11:2 (April 1993), 1-7.

[10] In a letter to me, John Biggs III says that "Father should have been familiar with *The Entailed Hat*," but doubts "that Father introduced Fitzgerald to it. Fitzgerald himself had good Maryland connections, certainly Baltimore (but not necessarily the Eastern Shore)" (November 8, 2003).

[11] Jerome R. Reich, in *Leisler's Rebellion: A Study of Democracy in New York, 1664-1720,* provides a detailed history of this episode from an appreciative point of view. Shields suggests that Townsend acquired some of his information about the Rebellion from *Valentine's Manuals*, City of New York, published circa 1821 (91). Also of interest is a play by Mrs. E. Oakes, *Old New York: or, Democracy in 1689—A Tragedy in Five Acts*, a melodrama about Leisler and Milbourne set on the day they were hanged.

[12] Townsend wrote under more than twenty pen-names, including not only "Gath," but also "G.A.T." and "Johnny Bouquet," we learn from Ruthanna Hindes's study (29). John Gault seems a natural choice for Biggs to have made in naming a character who in essential respects evokes Townsend's image. John Gault himself also uses a nom de plume, "Vanois" (Biggs 167, 170).

[13] *Demigods* and *Seven Days Whipping* were the only novels by John Biggs that were published. However, in a letter to Fitzgerald, Maxwell Perkins referred to a manuscript submitted by Biggs in 1929 that Scribner had rejected (Bruccoli and Duggan 233). Additionally, in February, 1920, Fitzgerald sent a manuscript copy of what must have been Biggs's first novel to H. L. Mencken to read (Bruccoli and Duggan 78). This could have been an early version of *Demigods*, or it could have been some other novel altogether—no title is mentioned in Fitzgerald's letter to Mencken. Biggs might, then, actually have written three novels or possibly four, though only two were published. However, Fitzgerald twice mentions a play by Biggs in letters to Maxwell Perkins during June, 1929, and November, 1929 (Turnbull, *Letters*, 238 and 240).

[14] Also see "The Fall of Utie" in Townsend's *Tales of the Chesapeake* (55). In it there is mention of a "Gadsby" who is a tavernkeeper. His tavern is mentioned, but he does not appear as a character.

[15] Nancy Milford records numerous instances of plagiarism by Scott Fitzgerald of his wife's writing; see the Index item in *Zelda*, "Zelda's diaries and letters used." Edmund Wilson and Arthur Mizener also mention Fitzgerald's debt to *Sinister Street*.

WORKS CITED

Biggs, John Jr. *Demigods*. New York: Scribner's, 1926.

Biggs, John III. Letter to David Meredith. November 8, 2003.

Bruccoli, Matthew J., and Margaret M. Duggan, eds., with the assistance of Susan Walker. *Correspondence of F. Scott Fitzgerald*. New York: Random House, 1980.

Clark, Charles B., ed. *The Eastern Shore of Maryland and Virginia*. 3 vols. New York: Lewis Historical Publishing, 1950.

Fact Sheets. Snow Hill MD : Furnace Town Foundation, 1998.

Fitzgerald, F. Scott. *The Great Gatsby*. New York: Scribner's, 1925.

Hindes, Ruthanna. *George Alfred Townsend: One of Delaware's Outstanding Writers*. Wilmington DE: Hambleton P, 1946.

Johnson, Christiane. "*The Great Gatsby*: The Final Vision." *Critical Essays on F. Scott Fitzgerald's The Great Gatsby*. Ed. Scott Donaldson. Boston: G. K. Hall, 1984. 112-17.

Mencken, H. L. "[Review of] *The Great Gatsby.*" *F. Scott Fitzgerald: The Man and His Work.* Ed. Alfred Kazin. New York: World Pub., 1951. 88-92.

Meyers, Jeffrey. *Scott Fitzgerald: A Biography.* New York: Harper, 1994.

Milford, Nancy. *Zelda.* New York: Harper, 1970.

Mizener, Arthur. *The Far Side of Paradise: A Biography of F. Scott Fitzgerald.* New York: Vintage, 1959.

Reich, Jerome R. *Leisler's Rebellion: A Study of Democracy in New York: 1664-1720.* Chicago: U of Chicago P, 1953.

Roulston, Robert. "Something Borrowed, Something New: A Discussion of Literary Influences on *The Great Gatsby.*" *Critical Essays On F. Scott Fitzgerald's The Great Gatsby.* Ed. Scott Donaldson. Boston: G. K. Hall, 1984. 54-66.

Seldes, Gilbert. "New York Chronicle." *Fitzgerald's The Great Gatsby: The Novel, the Critics, the Background.* Ed. Henry Dan Piper. New York: Scribner's, 1970. 125-26.

Shields, Jerry, ed. *GATH's Literary Work and Folk and Other Selected Writings of George Alfred Townsend.* Wilmington DE: Delaware Heritage P, 1996.

Smith, E. Oakes. *Old New York; or Democracy in 1689— A Tragedy in Five Acts.* New York: Stringer and Townsend, 1853.

Townsend, George Alfred. *The Entailed Hat, or Patty Cannon's Times: A Romance.* 1880. Cambridge MD: Tidewater, 1955.

--- *The Entailed Hat.* Ed. Hal Roth. Vienna MD: Nanticoke, 2000.

--- *Tales of the Chesapeake.* 1880. Cambridge MD: Tidewater, 1968.

Turnbull, Andrew, ed. *The Letters of F. Scott Fitzgerald.* New York: Scribner's, 1963.

Wilson, Edmund. "Fitzgerald Before *The Great Gatsby*." *F. Scott Fitzgerald: The Man and His Work.* Ed. Alfred Kazin. New York: World Pub., 1951. 77-81.

About the Author

David Meredith was born and reared in Cambridge on the Eastern Shore of Maryland. As a child he heard about Patty Cannon and how the lay of her house (one side of it in Maryland and the other side in Delaware) helped her avoid arrest for kidnapping Blacks and selling them South. On Sunday outings his family often paused for a while in front of this landmark, or admired the impressive old colonial house in Princess Anne where GATH's fictional Judge Custis is supposed to have lived, or inched down a rutty lane to the Nassawongo Iron Furnace near Snow Hill, all of which landmarks figure in George Alfred Townsend's The Entailed Hat. Some years later Meredith found a battered copy of this novel by Townsend at a library book sale and read it through, lingering in horror over the chapters about Patty Cannon and her gang. Only fairly recently he read John Biggs's Demigods and began to see correspondences between Biggs's novel and Hat, and between both of them and Fitzgerald's The Great Gatsby. The outcome is this critical essay, "Gatsby, GATH, and Gault."

Meredith, a retired Associate Professor of English, lives in Kent, Ohio. His degrees are a BA from Western Maryland College (now known as McDaniel College), an MA from Pennsylvania State University, and a PhD from Kent State University. Besides his dissertation, "Borrowing and Innovation in Five Plays by Aphra Behn," he has published an article on Elizabeth Bowen's "Ann Lee's" (in <u>Massachusetts Studies in English</u>, 8:2), five items in <u>A Dictionary of British and American Women Writers, 1601-1800</u>, ed. Janet Todd (1985), and several poems. While teaching at Kent, he wrote and edited the newsletter <u>Regional Report</u> for five years. He also represented Kent State University on two year-long faculty exchanges, one at Karl-Marx University in Leipzig, GDR, and the other at Aristotle University in Thessaloniki, Greece.